BULLYING DEFINED

Introduction: There are three types of bullying: Physical, Verbal and Relational (sometimes called Emotional). In the past decade, another form of bullying has become widespread; it's called Cyberbullying. In the definitions below, there are several key words that will help you identify bullying actions.

BUL•LY•ING

- When one person **repeatedly** and **intentionally** hurts another person with physical actions or words
- When a person with **more power** or **status** (i.e. physically stronger or more popular) **intentionally teases, taunts or hurts someone's feelings** or **repeatedly excludes** him or her
- When a person **takes someone else's property without permission**
- When a person **repeatedly threatens** another person

CY•BER•BUL•LY•ING

- When one person **spreads lies or rumors** about another person **online**, through text messages, email or social media sites such as Facebook or Twitter
- When a person **posts embarrassing pictures or mean comments** about another person on social media sites such as Twitter, Facebook or Instagram
- When a person **repeatedly teases or threatens another person online**, through instant messages, email, texts, or on social media sites

Note that while these definitions describe <u>one</u> person bullying another, sometimes a <u>group of people</u> "gang up" to bully a person.

LET'S BE CLEAR: WHAT BULLYING IS AND WHAT IT IS NOT.
BULLYING HAS 3 PARTS:

1 BEHAVIOR

Mean or hurtful behavior with the **intention** to harm another person

VOCAB WORD:

"Intentionally" – On purpose

2 FREQUENCY

The bullying behavior happens **repeatedly** over a period of time

VOCAB WORD:

"Repeatedly" – happens more than once; a frequent pattern of behavior

3 TARGET/VICTIM

The person who is bullied

VOCAB WORD:

"Target" – the person being bullied; bullies often choose their target because he or she is alone, weaker, younger or smaller, for example

WHAT BULLYING IS <u>NOT</u>:

Q: Is it bullying if someone is mean ONCE?
A: No. Bullying is when one person <u>repeatedly</u> picks on another person (or many people). Bullying may happen every day or every week, for example.

Q: Is it bullying if someone just wants to be alone or chooses another best friend:
A: No. Bullying is <u>intentionally</u> being mean or harmful.

LEARN HOW YOU CAN HELP STOP BULLYING!

TABLE OF CONTENTS

4   Why Talk About Bullying?

5   Bullying Defined

6   What Bullying IS... and is NOT

8   How Does It Feel?

9   Key Words

10   Word Match

11   The Bullying Scene

12   Bullying Facts

14   Be An Upstander, Not A Bystander

16   Poem and Self-Reflection Questions

20   Express Yourself

22   The Four R's

27   Myth-Busters

29   The Four-Step S.T.O.P. Method

31   Not To My Face – Cyberbullying

33   Bullying Awareness Campaign

36   Personal Pledge

38   Sources/Resources

WHY DO WE NEED TO TALK ABOUT BULLYING?

Introduction: Research shows that 90 percent of students in grades 4 through 8 report being victims of bullying, and nearly 50 percent of students say they have been bullied *online*. The majority of middle school students agree that bullying is a serious problem.

Kids who are bullied feel depressed, helpless and often afraid to go to school. And kids who are bullied online – on Facebook or Twitter or text messages – are up to 10 times more likely to consider suicide than non-victims, according to studies by Yale University.

The problem is growing. One of the most shocking facts is this one: *Every seven minutes, a student is bullied; 85 percent of the time, other students witness the bullying and nobody stops it.*

But now **you** have a chance to become more aware of bullying behavior and learn what you can do to help stop it.

IN THIS BOOK YOU WILL:

1. Learn a clear definition of bullying
2. Discover how to identify different types of bullying
3. Understand how bullying affects people
4. Learn a four-step plan to stand up to bullying
5. Read stories of bullying and make decisions about its harmful affects
6. Consider what you would do if you were being bullied
7. Work with your classmates to create an anti-bullying marketing campaign

Once you understand how harmful bullying is and what you can do to help stop it, we hope you will be part of today's movement to make schools safer for all children.

Q: ARE THERE DIFFERENT KINDS OF BULLYING?

A: YES, THERE ARE 4 KINDS:

1 PHYSICAL

Hitting, kicking, biting, pushing; also taking someone's property without permission

3 RELATIONAL/EMOTIONAL

Telling lies about someone; spreading rumors; excluding someone

VOCAB WORD:
"Exclude" – to leave someone out just to be mean

2 VERBAL

Name-calling, teasing, making fun of a person

4 CYBERBULLYING

A type of relational/emotional bullying

When bullying happens digitally, such as on social media sites, emails or text messages

Sources: The Journal of the American Medical Association. The U.S. Department of Education (DOE).

PEOPLE WHO ARE BULLIED OFTEN FEEL:

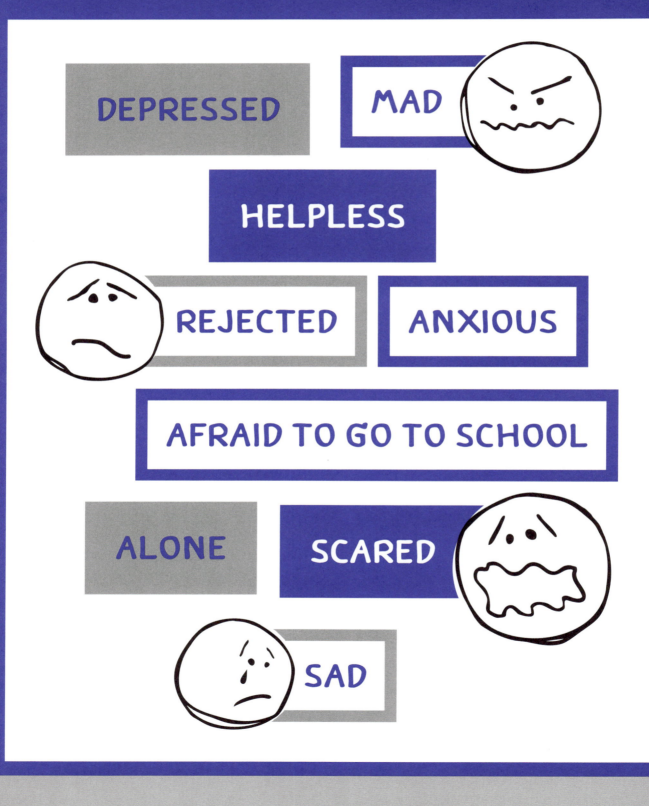

DEPRESSED

MAD

HELPLESS

REJECTED

ANXIOUS

AFRAID TO GO TO SCHOOL

ALONE

SCARED

SAD

ACTIVITY: KEY WORDS

Instructions: According to experts, there are several important words in the above definitions that help us clearly understand what bullying IS… and what it is NOT.

List three of these key words for bullying, and three for cyberbullying.

BULLYING DEFINED — 3 KEY WORDS:

1. _____

2. _____

3. _____

CYBERBULLYING DEFINED — 3 KEY WORDS:

1. _____

2. _____

3. _____

ACTIVITY: WORD MATCH

Instructions: Now that you have learned the definitions, key words and types of bullying, it is time to test your knowledge! Draw a line to match the word on the left with the definition on the right.

Damaging someone's property	Anxious
Constantly insulting someone	Exclude
To leave someone out just to be mean	Intentionally
Posting embarrassing pictures on Facebook	Verbal Bullying
The person who is being bullied	Target
Afraid all the time	Physical Bullying
On purpose	Cyberbullying

ACTIVITY: WRITE A BULLYING SCENE

Instructions: In this activity, imagine that you are the director of a television show about bullying. In the spaces below, write a scene that describes each type of bullying: physical, verbal, relational/emotional, and cyberbullying. Remember to include key words from the definitions.

Example: Describe a scene of physical bullying:

Every morning, Drew waits for Kevin in the hallway and pushes and shoves him against the wall. Sometimes Drew steals Kevin's lunch.

Now it's your turn.

1. Describe a scene of **PHYSICAL BULLYING**:

_____

_____

2. Describe a scene of **VERBAL BULLYING**:

_____

_____

3. Describe a scene of **RELATIONAL/EMOTIONAL BULLYING**:

_____

_____

4. Describe a scene of **CYBERBULLYING**:

_____

_____

HERE ARE SOME FACTS YOU SHOULD KNOW:

It is hard to stand up to a bully, because you may think the bully is stronger or braver than you are. The truth is, usually the bully is not very **confident** inside.

Half of all suicides among young people are related to bullying.

81% OF YOUNG PEOPLE THINK THAT IT IS EASIER TO GET AWAY WITH BULLYING ONLINE THAN IN PERSON.

68% OF TEENS THINK THAT CYBERBULLYING IS A SERIOUS PROBLEM.

Harassment and bullying have been linked to 75 percent of school shooting incidents.

Kids who bully think it will help them be "cool" or fit in – it doesn't.

EVERY SEVEN MINUTES, SOMEONE IS BULLIED ON A SCHOOL PLAYGROUND.

NEARLY 43% OF KIDS SAY THEY HAVE BEEN BULLIED ONLINE.

According to the National Center for Education Statistics, one out of four children is a victim of bullying. Over 3 million students are bullied each year.

Some students think that if they tell an adult that they are being bullied, it is considered "ratting someone out." It is not; it is the right thing to tell an adult you can trust to listen and support you.

KIDS WHO WITNESS BULLYING MAY KEEP QUIET BECAUSE THEY ARE AFRAID THEY WILL BE THE BULLY'S NEXT TARGET.

BULLYING IS NEVER OKAY.

Only 1 in 10 cyberbullied victims will tell a parent or trusted adult.

BE AN UPSTANDER, NOT A BYSTANDER

Introduction: Bullying is not just "kids being kids." It causes both physical and emotional pain. But it is not just the targets and bullies who are affected – students who **witness** bullying often feel helpless, ashamed or afraid that they will be the next target. If they don't speak up, they carry the burden of their guilt with them into adulthood, and that can cause anxiety or depression.

You can help prevent bullying in your school by choosing to be an "upstander," not a bystander.

BYSTANDER: Someone who sees bullying but "stands by" and doesn't do anything. A bystander witnesses a harmful situation but takes no action.

UPSTANDER: Someone who recognizes bullying and takes action, such as speaking up, helping the victim get out of the situation, or getting help from a trusted adult.

Instructions: Answer the questions below. Remember, there are no right or wrong answers, just your own thoughts and experiences.

DISCUSSION QUESTIONS:

Have you ever seen someone being bullied? Describe what you saw:

_____

_____

How did witnessing bullying make you feel?

_____

_____

BE AN UPSTANDER, NOT A BYSTANDER CONTINUED

What did you do in the situation?

_____

_____

_____

_____

Do you wish you had done something differently? If so, what? If not, why are you pleased with what you did?

_____

_____

_____

_____

_____

_____

_____

_____

As you become more aware of the effects of bullying through this activity book, what action would you take if you saw someone being bullied tomorrow?

_____

_____

_____

_____

POEM & SELF-REFLECTION QUESTIONS

Instructions: Read the poem below. How does the poem make you feel about the role of bystanders and upstanders? Answer the questions following the poem, referring to the stanzas indicated.

"TO LIVE ANOTHER DAY" BY G.D.E.

{1} It happens every morning
On the bus ride to my school;
I sit up front, invisible,
While "they" and "them" hold rule.

{2} The driver shouts a time or two
Before turning both blind eyes;
He doesn't lift a voice to help,
Though we hear the wretched cries.

{3} As class bells ring, more danger starts
Through hallways left and right.
I walk through fast, my head down low,
Not looking for a fight.

{4} I hear the noise – a bang! a slam!
A kid's against the wall.
He's surrounded by a bunch of guys --
They're huge and he's so small.

{5} I'm walking by, my mind a swirl,
Do I ignore it or assist?
Will they turn away? Will they turn on me?
Will their pummeling persist?

{6} If I do nothing now but keep my pace,
Is that not the same
As if I threw the punch, the kick?
As if I called the name?

{7} I catch the eye now of the boy
His need a silent cry.
Will I tell someone, or stay and shout?
Or just continue to walk by?

{8} I don't want to be a hero!
Or the next one that they choose.
I don't want to be a coward.
Seems like every way I lose.

{9} I don't want to be a "rat."
I don't want to be a friend.
But what if I choose nothing?
Aren't I as bad as them?

{10} So I slow my pace as I approach,
And with a voice that masks my fear,
I shout, "Hey stop it, man, he's just a kid."
I'm not sure that they hear.

{11} But by this time some other kids
Have gathered all around.
More shouts of "Stop!" and "That's not cool!"
We stand together, hold our ground.

{12} The others start to help the kid,
The bullies stride away.
I let out my breath and head to class
To live another day.

Instructions: Refer to the poem stanzas to answer the questions below.

1. What does the writer mean when he describes the bus driver as, "turning both blind eyes"? {Refer to stanzas 1 and 2.}

_____

_____

2. Why do you think the bus driver acts this way? {Refer to stanzas 1 - 2.}

_____

_____

3. The writer says that the bullies are "huge" and the target is "small." Why do you think bullies pick on weaker kids? What does that say about the bully? {Refer to stanza 4.}

_____

_____

4. Do you agree with the protagonist in the poem when he says, "But what if I choose nothing? Aren't I as bad as them?" Why or Why not? {Refer to stanza 6.}

_____

_____

5. Do you think telling a teacher would be considered "ratting" or "tattling?" Why or why not? {Refer to stanza 9.}

_____

_____

6. The protagonist says he doesn't want to be a "hero" or a "coward." Do you think these are accurate descriptions? Why or why not? {Refer to stanza 8.}

_____

_____

7. What would you have done if you were the student who witnessed the bullying?

_____

_____

8. What does the writer mean by "to live another day?" {Refer to stanza 12.}

_____

_____

EXPRESS YOURSELF

Instructions: Using words and pictures that you draw or cut out of magazines, create a collage that represents the harmful effects of bullying. Your artwork can be realistic, abstract or symbolic.

USE THE 4 R'S AGAINST BULLYING!

Introduction: Earlier lessons shared the definition of bullying and the many ways it effects people. But did you know that **YOU** have the power to help stop bullying from spreading in your school? Use the **4 R's!**

1. **RECOGNIZE** what bullying **IS**. Ask yourself about what you see:

    - Is one person physically hurting someone?
    - Is one person **OLDER** or **STRONGER** than the other person?
    - Does one person repeatedly pick on another person?
    - Is one person verbally or emotionally being mean **ON PURPOSE**?

If you answer "Yes" to any of these questions, you **RECOGNIZE** it **IS** bullying!

RECOGNIZE what bullying is **NOT**. Ask yourself about what you see:

- Are two friends simply arguing?
- Is one person just being bossy to other kids?
- Did someone tell a joke one time about another person?
- Did one person simply choose not to hang out or be friends with another person?
- Did someone have a party and just include a few close friends?

If you answer "Yes" to any of these questions, you **RECOGNIZE** this is **NOT** bullying. These describe everyday conflicts or choices that people sometimes make, without being intentionally or repeatedly mean.

Bullying Fact: Bully victims are up to 10 times more likely to consider suicide than non-victims, according to studies by Yale University.

Adapted from *Steps To Respect*, a curriculum from the Committee For Children www.cfchildren.org

2. **REFUSE** to be a "Silent Witness."

   - DO NOT be a "bully bystander." If a bully does not have people standing around watching, he or she might not act like a bully.
   - DO NOT be mean to someone just because someone else tells you to.
   - DO NOT laugh when someone tells a mean joke about another person.
   - DO NOT send or pass mean notes.
     (This goes for text messages, emails and Facebook posts, too.)
   - Do NOT be a "silent witness." If you see someone being bullied, speak up and tell a trusted adult.

3. **REJECT** being a bully victim.

   - If you think it is safe to speak to the bully, be calm and say, "Stop it. I don't like it when you talk to me that way."
   - Walk away <u>confidently</u>. (See self-confidence activity in your workbook).
   - Leave and go to where a friend is (or a group of friends).
   - If rejecting the bully doesn't work, and the bully continues, tell a trusted teacher, parent, coach, or other adult.

4. **REPORT** bullying!
   - If you are bullied or you see someone else being bullied, REPORT it.
   - Tell a teacher you trust, or a school counselor, or even the principal.
   - Talk to your parents or another family member – whoever you feel safe telling.
   - Make sure you ask someone to take action to help stop the bullying.

Bullying Fact: Many kids who are bullied are afraid to go to school. They stay home, miss school, and their grades suffer.

Adapted from *Steps To Respect*, a curriculum from the Committee For Children www.cfchildren.org

PUT THE FIRST "R" INTO ACTION: <u>RECOGNIZE!</u> IS THIS BULLYING?

Instructions: In this exercise, you'll decide if the scenarios on the following pages describe bullying or not. First, read these examples:

Example 1: Randi told Sarah she wanted to eat lunch by herself today.

Is this bullying? Yes (No)

Why or Why not?

Because Randi just wanted to be by herself. She was not being

mean to Sarah on purpose.

Example 2: Dedrick grabbed Sam's lunch and tossed it to a few other guys. Then he took the sandwich and ate it himself, just like he does every day.

Is this bullying? (Yes) No

Why or Why not?

Because Dedrick repeatedly steals Sam's property and is

intentionally mean to him.

NOW IT'S YOUR TURN!

Instructions: Read the following scenarios. Do you **RECOGNIZE** bullying or NOT?

Ask yourself the "**RECOGNIZE**" questions that you see around the border of the pages to help you decide.

1. Beth and Rachel got in a huge fight over a part in the school play. Everyone could hear them screaming at each other before they both stomped off.

   Is this bullying?   Yes   No

   Why or Why not?

   _____

   _____

2. Mike and Scott are on the football team together. Yesterday, Mike secretly followed Scott home from school. When they were a few blocks away, Mike jumped Scott and wrestled him to the ground. Mike told Scott if he skipped football practice again, he would beat him up.

   Is this bullying?   Yes   No

   Why or Why not?

   _____

   _____

ARE TWO FRIENDS SIMPLY ARGUING?

DID SOMEONE JUST WANT TO BE ALONE?

IS ONE PERSON OLDER OR STRONGER THAN ANOTHER?

3. Julie started dating a boy that Miriam liked. Miriam posted on Facebook that Julie "kisses everyone's boyfriend" and sent text messages to Julie that "everyone thinks you are ugly" and "you should just leave this school."

Is this bullying? Yes   No

Why or Why not?

_____

_____

4. During team practice, one of your teammates is always yelling from the sidelines for you to "run faster! Get to the ball! Stop hanging back!" It makes it hard for you to concentrate.

Is this bullying? Yes   No

Why or Why not?

_____

_____

You **can** learn to recognize bullying! When you see it, remember the rest of the **4 R'S**:

REFUSE to be a "Silent Witness"
REJECT being a bully victim.
REPORT bullying to a trusted adult

MYTH–BUSTERS

Instructions: Circle True or False for each of the statements below. See the following page for answers.

TRUE OR FALSE CHECKLIST

1. Bullying is just teasing.
   True   False

2. If two friends are arguing, it's not bullying.
   True   False

3. Almost half of all students say they have been bullied online.
   True   False

4. Bullying is just a phase kids go through.
   True   False

5. Most targets of Cyberbullying do not tell their parents.
   True   False

6. It's tattling to tell an adult when you're being bullied.
   True   False

7. Half of all suicides among young people are related to bullying.
   True   False

8. A majority of kids think that cyberbullying is a serious problem.
   True   False

Adapted from *The Bully Free Classroom: Over 100 Tips and Strategies for Teachers K–8*, by Allan L. Beane, Ph.D., professor in the special education department at Murray State University in Murray, Kentucky.

THE ANSWERS

1. **False.** Repeatedly teasing someone is a form of verbal bullying. Other types of bullying include physical violence, verbal threats, emotional exclusion, and Cyberbullying.

2. **True.** Sometimes friends disagree or even get into an argument; bullying is when one person is repeatedly and intentionally mean or cruel to another person.

3. **True,** according to a survey completed by iSafe America.

4. **False.** Bullying is not just a phase and it's not "normal." People who believe bullying is normal are less likely to tell an adult or stand up for a victim or themselves. It is not normal for someone to repeatedly insult, threaten, hurt or abuse another person.

5. **True.** According to the iSafe survey, 58% of kids did not tell their parents or an adult about being bullied online.

6. **False.** Telling an adult can help prevent or stop bullying, whether it's happening to you or someone else. It's smart to tell an adult you can trust to support you and take action.

7. **True.** According to the data analytics site, www.bullyingstatistics.org, teens who are bullied are 10 times more likely to commit suicide, and half of all youth suicides are related to bullying. No one can truly predict how a victim will respond to being bullied.

8. **True.** According to the anti-bullying campaign, *Do Something*, 68 percent of students surveyed agreed that cyberbullying is serious problem.

Adapted from *The Bully Free Classroom: Over 100 Tips and Strategies for Teachers K–8*, by Allan L. Beane, Ph.D., professor in the special education department at Murray State University in Murray, Kentucky.

THE FOUR–STEP S.T.O.P. METHOD

Introduction: It's good to have a plan so you know what you would do in case you are ever bullied, or if you see someone else being bullied. Here is an easy plan that has helped many students all over the country. It's called the **THE FOUR–STEP S.T.O.P. METHOD.**

S <u>S</u>TAND UP

for yourself. Say, "STOP it!" Say, "Leave me alone."
(Then walk away with <u>confidence</u>!)

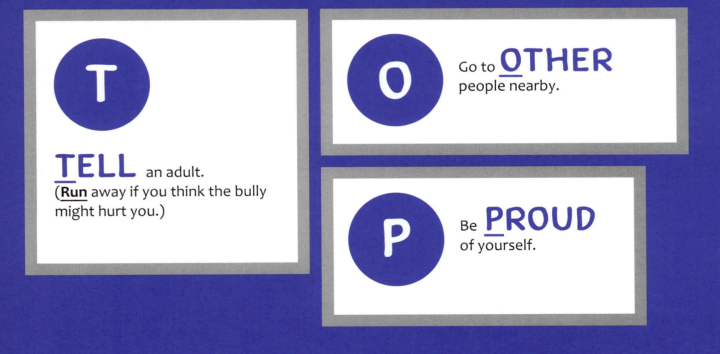

T <u>T</u>ELL an adult.
(<u>**Run**</u> away if you think the bully might hurt you.)

O Go to <u>OTHER</u> people nearby.

P Be <u>PROUD</u> of yourself.

THE FOUR-STEP S.T.O.P. METHOD: A DRAMATIZATION

Introduction: Your teacher will divide you into groups of four and ask you to write a short skit about bullying. Everyone in your group must participate in the skit, either by writing, directing and/or acting. Your skit must also appropriately use the four steps in the S.T.O.P. Method.

Once you have written your skit, practice within your group. Your teacher may ask your group to perform the skit for the class.

Use these questions to help you develop your S.T.O.P. Method skit:

- Where does the scene take place?
- Who are the characters?
- What type of bullying is it?
- What does the bully do and say?
- What does the target do and say?
- What does the adult in the skit do and say?
- What do the witnesses do and say?
- How does the target feel about his/her actions?

Bullying Fact: 6th graders are most vulnerable to bullying and cyberbullying. In a nationwide study, 90 percent of students in grades 4 through 8 report being victims of bullying.

NOT TO MY FACE — CYBERBULLYING

Introduction: This activity book provides a lot of important information about Cyberbullying (when a person is mean to someone online, such as posting threats, lies or embarrassing pictures on Facebook, or sending hurtful text messages). People who are cyberbullied often feel frightened, angry and helpless. Victims feel as if there is no way to escape the bullying because it happens online, often in their own home.

Because cyberbullies are not face-to-face with their victims, they don't see the victims' reactions or witness the pain and sadness that their actions cause.

Experts suggest that if you are being cyberbullied, you should:

- Tell a trusted adult, such as a parent or teacher.
- Copy and save the online posts or texts to show the trusted adult.
- Do not try to reason with the bully or tell your side of the story.
- Turn off your computer.
- Block the person from your cell phone so he/she cannot text you.
- If you see someone else being bullied online, do not join in or make any comment.

Spreading online rumors, gossiping and lies, and other forms of cyberbullying, are cruel, thoughtless actions that hurt people deeply – even if you don't see a wound or a scar. A good rule to live by is: **Never say anything online that you wouldn't want your grandmother to read.** When you participate in cyberbullying, you could be harming someone in a *fatal* way. Remember: Half of all suicides among young people are related to bullying.

1. How do you define Cyberbullying?

_____

_____

2. Do you think being mean online or gossiping online is just part of "school drama?" When does drama turn into Cyberbullying?

_____

_____

3. Why do you think people post mean words or embarrassing pictures of someone online or in texts?

_____

_____

4. Do you think one type of bullying is worse than another? Why or why not?

_____

_____

Bullying Fact: 1 out of every 10 students who drops out of school does so because of repeated bullying.

CAMPAIGN TO STOP BULLYING

Introduction: In this activity, YOU are the creative director of a marketing agency and YOU are in charge of creating a campaign to help stop bullying! What would your campaign look like? What would your slogan be? What drawings or pictures from magazines could you use? Here are some other campaign slogans to help you get started:

Designed by the agency Leo Burnett, Chicago, for Procter & Gamble, Secret Deodorant. © 2011

The anti-bullying campaign of the United Federation of Teachers (UFT), A Union of Professionals, in partnership with Respect for All.

An anti-bullying campaign from **DoSomething.org**, the U.S.'s largest not-for-profit for young people and social change.

ACTIVITY: MY ANTI–BULLYING CAMPAIGN

1. Decide: Who is your "target audience?" These are the people your campaign will focus on or speak to. Circle one or more.

   - Parents
   - Elementary school students
   - Middle school students
   - High school students
   - Bullies
   - Victims of bullying
   - Your community
   - The whole school

2. What is your "call to action?" What do you want people who read your campaign to **_do_**?

   - Stand up to bullying
   - Tell someone when they see bullying
   - Don't be a bully
   - Don't be a victim
   - Tell someone when they are being bullied
   - Learn more about the dangers of bullying

You may have other actions you want people to take, and that's great! It's YOUR campaign! Create yours on the following page.

Bullying Fact: Celebrities who were bullied include Lady Gaga (who was thrown in a garbage can), Rosario Dawson (for being flat-chested), Kate Winslet (for being chubby), and Michael Phelps (for his big ears).

MY ANTI—BULLYING CAMPAIGN

Write your slogan and call to action, then add your campaign copy and pictures.

Slogan: _____

Images

Call to action: _____

ACTIVITY: WRITE A PERSONAL PLEDGE

Introduction: A pledge is a promise you agree to and commit to uphold at all times. If you were going to make a pledge to help prevent bullying, what would you say? Sometimes writing our commitments helps us keep them.

Example Pledge Statements:

- I pledge not to bully.
- I will help others in need.
- If I see bullying I will report it.
- I will be kind to people who are different from me.
- Bullying of any kind is not okay with me.

Instructions: Now it's your turn to write your own pledge. Include any or all of the above statements that are important to you, and write a few of your own.

MY PLEDGE:

_____

_____

_____

_____

_____

_____

_____

_____

_____

CONGRATULATIONS!

YOU HAVE COMPLETED THE BULLYING AWARENESS STUDENT ACTIVITY WORKBOOK. YOU SHOULD BE PROUD OF YOUR COMMITMENT TO LEARNING MORE ABOUT BULLYING AND WAYS TO PREVENT IT. WITH YOUR NEW KNOWLEDGE AND UNDERSTANDING, WE HOPE THAT YOU WILL LIVE BY THE PLEDGE YOU CREATED AND HELP BE A LEADER IN THE EFFORT TO END BULLYING.

SOURCES/RESOURCES

Above The Influence National Campaign
www.abovetheinfluence.com

The Bully Free Classroom: Over 100 Tips and Strategies for Teachers K–8, by Allan L. Beane, Ph.D., professor in the special education department at Murray State University in Murray, Kentucky.

Bullying Statistics
www.bullyingstatistics.org/content/bullying-and-suicide.html

Common Sense Media
www.commonsensemedia.org

Connect with Kids, Inc.
www.Connectwithkids.com

Do Something National Campaigns
www.dosomething.org

www.Education.com

Focus on the Family
www.focusonthefamily.com

i-SAFE America, Inc.
www.isafe.org

Invisible Weapons Documentary and Resource Guide
Connect with Kids, Inc.

Josephson Institute, Center for Youth Ethics
www.charactercounts.org

The Journal of the American Medical Association
www.jama.jamanetwork.com/journal.aspx

Kamaron Institute, management and educational consulting firm a
www.kamaron.org/Cyber-Bullying-Articles-Facts

SOURCES/RESOURCES

National Crime Prevention Council website
www.ncpc.org/resources/files/pdf/bullying/cyberbullying.pdf

Pacer Center
www.pacer.org

Scholastic
www.scholastic.com

Silent Witness Resource Guide
Connect with Kids, Inc.

Sticks and Stones Resource Guide
Connect with Kids, Inc.

StopBullying.gov
www.stopbullying.gov

The Substance Abuse and Mental Health Services Administration (SAMHSA)
www.samhsa.gov

U.S. Department of Education
www.ed.gov

Us Magazine, "Stars Who Were Bullied"
www.usmagazine.com/celebrity-news/pictures/celebs-who-were-bullied-2010510/10462

STUDENT NOTES:

STUDENT NOTES:

STUDENT NOTES: